ANNA RABINOWITZ

Darkling

A POEM

ALSO BY ANNA RABINOWITZ

At the Site of Inside Out

ACKNOWLEDGMENTS

Grateful acknowledgment is made to the editors of the following journals where portions of *Darkling* first appeared:

Atlantic Monthly, B City, Boston Review, Denver Quarterly, Interim, LIT, Sulfur and *Volt*

Darkling

ANNA RABINOWITZ

Tupelo Press
Dorset, Vermont

Tupelo Press
PO Box 539
Dorset, VT 05251
802.366.8185 • fax 802.362.1883
editor@tupelopress.org • web www.tupelopress.org

for Ethan Samuel Longenecker
Rachel Laurel Friedman
Avery Samuel Friedman

Beyond generations
(January 1, 2000)

Ruth Chernoff

This is to c...
...no...
...issued...

...assport is issued. In witness whereof,
...e seal of the Department of State is
...pressed thereon.

Hair _____ *Brown*

Eyes _____ *blue*

Distinguishing marks or featu[res]

_____

_____

Place of birth _____ *Poland*

Date of birth _____ *Feb.*

Occupation _____

_____

Ruth Cher[...]

Signatur[e]

For we are but of yesterday, and know nothing,
because our days upon earth are a shadow...
Job 8:8

Nobody is ever missing.
John Berryman

Then there is a time in life when you just take a walk.
And you walk in your own landscape.
Willem deKooning

The word moves a bit of air and this the next until it reaches
the ear of one who hears it and is therein awakened.
Nachman of Bratslav

It was not stillness for that is the mere absence of noise, but
it was silence which means that those who kept silence
could, apparently, have spoken if they had pleased.
Leonid Andreyev

And how will you enquire, Socrates, into that which you
do not know? What will you put forth as the subject of
enquiry? And if you find what you want, how will you ever
know that this is the thing which you did not know?
Meno

Bear with me for singing their song
They are not here to sing
They did not want to sing

Inside: a story —
                    inventories, incidents —
                            pleading to be flossed
                    from the teeth of silence —

Leaching congealed vowels
                    lately of / longing for / words —

Explanations not yet factored into claim: —
                                    this is this —
                    that is that —

As in first annunciations / as in debuts
                    for old roles /

                    as if to atone:
                                    yes, I love you —

Namers courting drifting sands,
                    fated to root heels,
Toes into dunes rampant with consonants of
Unreachable destinies,

                    lonely nouns of hearts
Pilgriming to wished-for places
                    on the verbs
Of desire —
                    destinations where nothing feels
New but an aching need to shout out.

Again and again the narrative howls for words.

Circling, leaping into
                    / out of / shade, but it makes
Only wrong turns —
                    how can it say the right thing? — shall it

Pledge never to do that again,
            to be good next time?

            — a daughter /
Parents —
            blooms at the edge of a small scream —

In the beginning is the end — words and more buds —
            fingers knotted / throats
Choked —
            syllables scuffling for a spot / patient for a time

Entropies, upstretched vacancies,
                              delays
Grazing sound —
            too soon for /
                  in the aftermath of / being —

Amok with what is unseen / unsaid: *love me,*
Touch me, make use of me —

            preludes

                  as in dawnings,

      distances

                  as in prayers

Ensnared at the main gate —

                  and now —

                  and now—

                        oh god —

                  they're dead.

Why does it end like this? No word, no
Hand across the lines, no bridge or rope,
                    only a boulder at the
Eleventh hour
                    (which is forever)
                              rolling uphill —

Note bene: a daughter,
First of your flesh — loved you — she loved you —

Right to the end, she loved you, but could not shape the sound
Of it, as if the sound of it had been worn out
Struggling to get one step ahead of her scream
                    when you wouldn't sit down
To a meal without being prodded,
                    when there seemed no
Way to know whether you wished to come or go, when
Amends needed always to be pressed into
Service, and the job description declined to be defined.

Silted lakes of memory — out-of-focus yesterdays
Pile up aimlessly (recklessly?), as if to claim
Enigma as the source (goal?) of experience, to quash
Curtailed scenes in which queries were packed away,
The troved treasure of histories closed,
Reduced to an index of footnotes bereft of a text.

                    Then one day it is too late to
Enroll in the old course which exists to retrieve
Great books, and one evening
              it becomes a consciousness-
Raising session — all the inmates
Apostled to a little love, a little respect.

              Is that what you hoped for too, Mama — all
You ever really wanted out of it?

And that time — that hard winter — the El quaking on its tracks,
Narrowly logging distances, station to station, to confirm the hands-
Down drive to get there, the sooner the better, (better late than never?).
We shot out, eyes glazed with intensity, high-fired windowpanes crazed
In the glare for which late afternoon pleads guilty, while
Night, making its daily round, pulled down the sun, and
Tunneled into the dark center of itself. Oh, how we tore into the
Envelope of evening. *Dear God, do not deliver us unto evil. Help us*
Recover the lost boy — only three, blond, blue-eyed, wearing his
Scarlet hat with the white angora stripe, and his leggings —
Dark brown, like mud-slogged Gravesend Bay, its grime
Rambling into the roots of a few plane trees unleafed near the
Edge of the shore. *This day, this day, big sister, your job was to stand*
Guard, not to turn away — not even for a minute — not a second —
Sister, daughter, darling girl, light of this life, why? — What
Made you look the other way — long enough for him, oh delicious
Apple of their tree, to disappear?— Benson Avenue, Bay 26th, 28th, up,
Down, in, out, alleys, basements, doorways, frenzy of feet, desperate air
Etherizing in throats. *The child? Where is the child?* — Oh, deadly
Dream drenched with their lives! And nightpities coursing on
Eagle's wings…

        Then, the precinct station a mile away — his face
Striped with tears, and the childless old woman who held
Out her hand, nestled him home for milk, and delivered him into the
Long arm of the law.

        What happened? — a bad seed, wanting
          little brother purged from her life —

    no, no!

A story afloat with the last
Threads of time —

      one scene in the plot —

        marks are made

          they don't

Erase

There — over there — beside the iron fence,
Holding on, holding on,

Each cell of her flesh a clear crystal
Waiting for a cut — which could be another facet of
Experience in the life ahead — or a crack —
A flaw in what comes next — or to *cut out* though she doesn't
Know yet about
Exits —

Nor does she know cousins, aunts, uncles, grandparents
In the old country will be gassed in a few years — and she will
Never have spoken with them, never have touched them or smelled
Garlic on their breaths. She doesn't know as she poses how camera
Expertise negates the future and absolves the past, that her play-
　　　　　ground
Yellows while rutabagas rot in distant basements and extraordinary
Events ooze poison — against reason, against history — houses, fields
Outraged by fire — blue claws of flame strangle foreign premises.
Final solutions are at hand while official denials spangle the airwaves.

Dear child of the snapshot taken in Brooklyn — eternally in place,
Arms wrapped around your Polish doll —

　　　　　　　of the *there* that is nowhere —

You, burning to get out — to scald the world with reasons to be.

There's been a slippage,

                        slow ricochet into blear, as if

History refuses to reveal its presence in the scheme, its
Eternal *being* in that verge

                  — *being* or *pending* —

Tangled bindweed in the debris of what has occurred.

Acres of fact occupy the
No-man's land I had hoped to explore.
Grass is not greener there, but it grows
Like crazy. And it's so hard to find the stepping stones.

Elsewhere is a long way away.

Dust crackles there and I
Believe the fountains have gone underground
In the time it has taken me to get here, which is
Not near at all.

Every step becomes more demanding.

Sequence is the crux of the game despite
Talk brewing in the marketplace about chaos,
Entropy, black holes, and the like.

Meanwhile, I must not forsake
Scrawls on my slate —
Scores of music I
Can't hear any more,
Or won't listen for because I'm afraid to
Relive those old mistakes.
Everywhere there are rhythms to be
Drummed, notes to be
Thrummed in this incurable
Hiddenness, but how does one get in when
Entry seems always blocked?

        Never mind, there are no
Surprises, no secrets, at least not for my
Kin, not in these *fin-de-millennium* years when no money buys
Yesterday and tomorrow's rage storms today, rife with the dark.

Late resorts among frayed echoes,
                              dissolves out of shadowrange —

I must find a path in this stupefying darkness that insists we
Knuckle down to its relentless advances —
Even when we hope against hope for reprieve —
Solace for a change.

That's not to say there's no time for joy,
                              even a custom-colored dream or two.

Rest assured, it can happen—
                                        in the lure of a day,
In the time it takes to shake a fist or
Nod hello — but for me there's the steady
Groan, a motor in my ear — which may be
Synonymous with on-goingness or going on —

                                        going on with
One's life knowing, though it dribbles like
Farina down an infant's chin,
                              it can be —   no!
                              it *is* truer than art.

But what is Life? And what is Art?

                          — such big questions!

Reader, I've set them aside in order to concentrate
On finding the Past
               if it's still there.

                     I want to
Knock at its gate when I'm least expected —
                         catch it off guard,
Even undressed, maybe on its way to bed —

                     just as it puts its spectacles on the
Night table and leans over to tell Life how much it
Loves it —
               before it rolls over to flick off the lights.
You have no idea how sure I am of those two —
Relying on one another every minute, shuffling into, out of
Each other's skins, draped in sheer magnitudes,
Sleeping and waking as if eternity scapes the shift of a lid.

As if a pen's breathprint clears heartlands where the
Nearly nulled rise like saplings from the austere
Drive of an unsummoned earth...

As if all this thinking restores the dead, undead, at
Last replanted in the foreground, stolid, multi-trunked oaks
Leafing into the fraught season, newborn in a green time...

Meaning no longer in memoriam in this city of black
Avenues, sirens in the clouds, buildings so tall and
Narrow that passing through is subject to foreclosure...

Kaleidoscopes, tesserae, residue of the raked up, scraped
Into, taken for granted, left to molder: mulch for
Nothing within earshot or embrace...

Dappled gleanings: begonias gone leggy in the heat,
Targlare from roofs of taxpayers below, sedum
Heeled in in the Sicilian's backyard, the radio:

A girl from Virginia coal country married
To an English earl — soap opera pitched to a heart-
Hunger, happy endings packaged for a move...

As if to bolt away is to forget, to plunge into the
Unfurled arms of a world where the ethnic can be denied —
No longer sting in the veins — immigrant parents, greenhorns...

The overbrimmed loneliness, downpour of being without,
Exorbitance fixed on families: grandparents, aunts, uncles, even
Distant cousins — everyone had one but me...

Newsreels: how I searched for a face, a name to moor
In my here and now — here and now, then and
Gone — this urgency to mark up emptiness from street to
Highway, from womb of clouds to unhatched sea.

Heel and toe. Is that the way back to raw footage?

Awkward states of being stumble through scattershot clips —
Documents of *was* appear as
Shards back then when seasonal myths made offerings
On location — known quantities hoping to make sense of the plot.

Understand: the bric a brac of opening scenes keeps
Going nowhere:
               she: crouched at the sewing machine,
Hands guiding a seam's lean course...huddled as if
Trapped in the down of the sofa...anchored side-saddle on
The kitchen chair...stooped at the stove cupping scum from the broth.
He: asleep, feet reeking like decayed potatoes in the corner store...
Each day the basement bakeshop...his hollow chest...
               his water eyes less full, more pale...

Is this the place for a cut?
               no, not yet. Other frames:
                          grapes ferment on the fire escape, seeded
Rolls rise in the coal-fired oven, hot tea cools in the glass.
He has worked hard, all his life worked so hard there's been no
Opportunity for an inventory, no chance *to be...to be...*

Understand: there's just enough to put
Supper on the table, no surplus for Sunday dinner at the Famous.

Economy tugs at the screen...remnants are cautiously cut,
               then stitched into shirts and skirts.

How am I doing? any progress?

        or does this proceed in an
Ongoing endured as beginnings dressed in
Leitmotifs of a vanished past
              filtered through lenses
Darkly...barely at all?

        just once...   no! let's make it
Forever...I've got to replay
It...   right or wrong, I've got to get it
Real again in this now-or-never situation — all the
Exposures, encounters, accountings,
            the episodes on film...
Silent performances,
        round as her face
           as it zooms into focus,
              full as the moon
           he traced on the rug with a cane.

KARTKA POCZTOWA

W-ny

...rnowin

...strołęka

...zien Łomż

50.000.000

Three weeks earlier they'd met and married — then she fled —
sailed off in a
Huff — and winds whinnied through the ship —
and star-
Entangled *whys* pocked the fictive fields of sea.

Did she lament as she
Lay on her berth at the bottom of the boat?

Would she explain
Afterwards?

She As She Was, "I as I am," racing to become
Native to herself.

Because he had jibed, "Your face folds up,
Dissolves, purses, puckers, crimps like a dry
Sponge." —

Why? Why had they married?

Swarms of bees cruised the canopy above their
Heads. Three fiddles whined under a gibbous moon,
A maverick sea, harbors kicking up their feet,
Roared like a cannon down the corridors of their bones.

Passage to America.

Was it for that? Or not to be alone
For even a minute more? Or to live in a six-story walk-up, to
Earn a hand-to-mouth wage, to bury the corpse of their dreams,
Always to feel alien, one foot here, the other in the old country?
Tasting the difference, each day starved for the leftover plate, but
Unable to eat — trapped in a cage of whose making? — two children
Reaching for bread —

                         so how does she
Enter her life? What wings will jab
Sharp shoals of light?
                    Whose feathers flare the sun?

                    Alone, at night,
She will not, cannot sing.

Every day he waits for a letter.

Every day she fails to write.

"My dearest," he scrawls, "remember our walks in the woods,
Evenings we bathed in the cold stream...how we shivered..."

"Dear husband," she replies, "I am not beautiful, my eyes
Tuck into my cheeks. I will not bleed when you speak, I am neither
Opus nor brief text, I am not scarf around your neck, nor
Beard at your chin. I am me,

                    I am *me* —
                              the one I'm
Expected (entrusted) (enabled) to be...

          (AND WHO IS THAT, WHO IS THAT?)

               They must not ask me:

Woman, why were *you* not *you*?"

"They will not ask me why I was not Sarah; they will not
Hunger for Leah or Rachel, but O, the
Endless speculation about why I walked
Cautiously inside your footprints, why
Each day a different me strode into my
Name — struggling to claim herself…"

                              Deep-eyed, Stub-
Toer of the Mark

Undoer of the Words —

                    undulation, ululation in the brain —

                              ten thousand caves
Rivered with inscriptions —

                              "what made me cower before
Your strides?"

Say it wasn't so — say it wasn't so —

"Chains break at the gaping link —
Orphaned, unfledged, unable to read the glyphed walls,
Rent by the lateness of answers approaching my throat..."

Propagator of Exile

                          Shaper of Inaction

Spurner of Roots

Ecrivaine of Independence

             Hostage to a Book of Half-hoped Pages

Orphan of Despair

Unable to say...

                 year after year

Thirsting to say...

               "ENOUGH."

Like felons, words can be reprieved, false starts remade. Tell me
Even now it's not too late —

A troop of mouths is on the march — and each sound
Narrowly derails oblivion — O truce of
Tongues, break ranks,

                       toll...   toll...

Hamburg, 1928.
                    "My ship sets sail," she writes.

Into marmoreal syllables — veiny
Silence of anotherworld, anothertime —

        Before technicolor and TV,
        before goosesteps mated with Heil,
        before numbered forearms and yellow stars,
        before "Whistle While You Work" and "I've Got
        My Love To Keep Me Warm" —

        "Hundreds in steerage
Cram the decks. I sleep on foul-smelling straw
Rammed into filthy ticking, eat gruel and stale bread;
        every night I toss on my cot, wrestling
        God-Knows-What,
        the Atlantic clubbed by rapid
Yaws and rolls to anotherlife, anotherchance."

        Before Zyklon B, before Hiroshima. In the year
        of teleprint and teletype, Romberg's "New Moon"
        and Lang's "Woman On the Moon," "Strange
        Interlude," penicillin and "Button Up Your Overcoat" —

        "Still, we have good times. Joseph, the cantor,
Presses two fingers to the base of his
Throat and unfurls a skein of falsetto notes."

Trills no longer sound, a ship no longer shape,
        scenes no longer playable,

                            yet,

Had I lived this —

        even then —

Everything would be missing —

                       even so —

stalking the unpossessable,
entreating the impalpable —

I would forage through Nothingness —

in case —

in

Case —

even then —

by figment or fragment —

it was there

"His songs are echoes of an echo of an echo...
I listen and I long for what will happen next."

— cause, effect, inspections for
Lice —

last looks —

Old valises splintered apart,
mica-dazzled, dreamed-
Up boulevards of a golden land —

which is America — which is where
they are heading — which is where
she will wear herself out —

Doing, undoing —

but wait, wait!
by the knot of the tongue,
by the pit of the eye, the ear churns
Yesterday —

and she is singing out her lungs —

and she will season her eyes with streets
teeming with emptiness,

squander her heart in tenements
reeking of ungrateful walls,

and she will weary her ears with insatiable
tickings of unattained goals,
file her teeth on wild wires
of sirengrief,
silence her mouth

with itineraries ground to a halt at the limits of bones —

and she will disembark in a strange
Country not knowing all history is an epitaph spinning
Away from her — an appetite unable to fix invisibles — a stutter
between two voids — expendable as
Nevermore readings, inaccurate as the peripatetic mind —

Obsessive Ruminator About the Once-of-Was —
Paraphraser of Ages and Ages Ago —

grieving for lack of insight,

Yearning for congruities, disparities — re-views, old views —
any news:

a bird of the air to carry the voice and
that which has wings to tell the matter —

half-tones in half-dark...

Tentative gropings for kernels of *was*...
        memory-shucked husks of history:

His bed in Warsaw: a pine plank between two wooden chairs...
        his workday: eighteen hours to learn a trade:
Eggs beaten pale, lumps of dough rising to buns and rolls...

Weekly Bund meetings where he sits riveted:
        Help lies in us alone...unity increases power...

                        under a single flag...

In a single hope...

        We must go out face to face with a mighty arm...

Name me Gatherer of Seed.

Daylight, twilight, nightlight, history shoulders everything —
        and nothing,
Heir to its own disillusion (dissolution) — offering up winters
        as they may *not* have been —
Insatiable accruals of query and claim:

        antonyms,
                as in that which jars (bars) memory,
Synonyms:
                as in renegade clues.

                    Believe me,
                        I have seen them
Devoured,
                heard them silenced by their own
Entropies...

        minuends from which everything is subtracted —

                  Believe me,
            history can be neither bought,
        nor stolen, nor faked,

neither borrowed nor slaked —

Adream on his chairs, he is lonely and prays for her letter.

              Believe me,
Thousands of instances, images crouch in that alterworld
        where random rhymes of time release flocks of vowel
Having no truck with air, making no sound of fact,

Lost coveys of consonants with clipped wings —

And he dreams, and he waits, and he breaks bread
        in a two-room flat where eight of them sleep.

                     Believe me, this
Must be told because it is foreign to me.

Everywhere feathers leap from the dust and, powerless
        before them, I must take
Note of their pleas to be gathered: first
Thoughts seeking a second life, long-distance
        flyers ready to live a double death...

Thesis: black holes / white holes / wormholes / origin and
          fate — they'll last me a lifetime sans regret:
      what I know I cannot know, I need not forget.

Hypothesis: prior translations sprout on scattered tongues;
          hear me's moss in bloodless mouths: what they
      didn't want to remember, I'm unable to forget.

Ein Sof: root of all roots: cause of all causes: unreadable,
          unknowable, except to itself: speaker in numbers:
      what I cannot know, I must not forget.

A priori: an infant universe of ten dimensions once ripped apart:
          remaindered: reality: three dimensions plus time:
      a man, a woman, dimensionless, crossed the sea to forget.

Note bene: they include time yet they are timeless: they contain
          the world, but the world would not contain them;
      what I've come to note, I must not forget.

Cosmology: the world is names, the names numbers: Isaac the Blind,
          unfettered by terrestrial eyes, saw ten digits without end:
      how do I quote names I can neither recall nor forget?

Insight: chapters locked in time: shredded Torah scrolls,
          sacks of flour poured on the road, posterities of pine
      flamed to ash: I've come to know; I must not forget.

Empirical: what is admissible: her knee nudging
          the sewing machine lever, his gun-shot leg:
      that which must be scavenged, because we forget.

Numerology: arms assembling / reassembling: number my
          stars: number my grass: number my blood: earth
      deafened by ciphers indecipherably quiet.

Themes: the narrative reveals hints of what it was / is / should /
          could have been: their sisters and brothers read
      haven anywhere: even remote islands chose to defect.

Premise: black holes roam enfoldments deeper than fears
        trapped in their eyes: never-to-be-known
    scenarios sentenced to decomposed alphabets.

Understand: I am trying to get to the bottom of things;
        I am trying to open the folds, to unroll the bolts;
    I am trying not to forget.

Leitmotifs: this meal with the foretaste and aftertaste
        of not knowing: these entrées sautéed in unbuttered
    sounds: this meat-starved, chipped-plate banquet.

Sixth sense: Safed: in the presence of absence, saying little, intending
        much, Isaac ben Solomon Luria spoke to the speechless
    birds: black are the holes' cavities, awesome the glister of jet!

Ergo: we die into life; we live into death; printouts
        torn and seamed, ravelled and patched:
    nothing is chaste.

Ontology: hollow bowls (graves) of *when* beneath crazed plates(fields)
        of *where* beside empty cups (houses) of *why*:
    their tables were set.

Further-
more: they wrote letters begging to be read, and got no reply;
        pried open windows of windowless rooms, rubbed out
    their eyes with failures of light; swallowed gruel and grit.

Gnostic
moan: why did you forsake them: why did you retreat
        from your witness sky, your righteous world unbuilt?:
    must their candles perish because they're unlit?

Epistem-
ology: theirs is not stillness unnoised; theirs is silence exiled from
        sounds of uncountable generations: theirs is language
    with the grammar beaten out of it.

Rationale: because they inhaled the air, because they exhaled the air,
        because they occupied space, slept and ate and walked
    streets, because their eyes were green, blue, sometimes violet…

Mandate: *see to it that nothing is lost or forgotten...record...and collect!*
             but their history was ending, their families erased:
             they sealed their lips and left me to imagine what to forget.

Affirmation: let the poverty of my words not be abject; let them
              persist in making and remaking, shaping, reshaping:
              to name, rename, unname: not to forget.

Nomen-   for a world never to be repeated, only to be archived:
  clature: trying-to-enter-the-thing, trying-to-name-the-loss words;
             survival not as a desire, but as a duty to celebrate.

Destiny: *a community in the van of the East...a land set for a halting-*
               place of enmities, a neutral ground...wilderness become
             a pool of water and the land no longer termed *desolate.*

Belief: they didn't believe in God; nor that they were chosen
               as models for the gentiles; they understood suffering,
             otherness: tattered clothes: how well they came to fit.

Inquiry: why? was it because their language was never spoken
               by anyone with power, the only tongue without
             a vocabulary for war: merely howls and ash to record it?

Rebuttal: *when you have a great and difficult task...if you only work*
               a little at a time...without faith and without hope, suddenly
             the work will finish itself. But will it be free and I free of it?

Tautology: singing your song without singing your song:
               dashes, dots, commas, deflected threads splicing air:
             to disclose what it would impoverish me to forget.

Hypothesis   what I know is what I need to unknow and reknow:
  cum plea: a sea of syllables frightening to swim,
             bent on utterance before I forget.

Wheeling, writing — lunatic particulars condemned to event —
And evidence

/ layer upon layer /

impossible to view through the swollen fog —

Signs later to be deplored / repudiated /
Stashed away in a corner of the closet…

Her father: writing from a deep cave of pain:
"why, why did you
Run off so soon after the wedding without saying goodbye?"

a morning her brother pleads, *"take me along,"*
an afternoon his cousin flees Warsaw for the woods,
the night they fathom unthinkable
sayings said,

Undoable doings done —

Hier ist kein Warums skittering willy
Nilly over the skin of the Vistula / charging at them /
forcing them to their
Knees as the not-yet-disclosed claws at the shore:

and more —

who foresees diabolic
Epilogues in the crowded square,
surrender when the notice
to round up Jews is nailed to the doors,
howls curdling in throats as the
Nominal becomes fact

and tanks memorize the dirt roads, quote
Houses,
end-stop fields,
drive tire-tread finales into their eyes —

After all / *no one knew / no one believed / it could be like that* —

Reader, reflect on this: retreaters from the narrative:
              emigrés: a husband, a wife, faces turned away

                           then he sails back —

Dapper, newly American, pants pleated and cuffed — in
A yellowed photo poses on the porch,
                        eyes
Narrowed over threads of smoke —

                 sails back with a sister's
Dowry to hire the musicians, arrange for the feast —

                    while she — (abandoned) —

Drums her fingers on a table in Brooklyn, two children in tow,
Rife with *why me's* and *if only's*

Yoked to an untranslatable syntax — the walls of her world
              peeling — layer after layer —
                parsing griefs

Amplitudes of silence and pleas to be inscribed for a good year —
                avalanche of pride groveling for survival —
                dread and allure of her deep eyes —

Narratives to be believed / doubted / stumbled upon —
Dreamed up/ into / out of —
                                at odds with themselves —
                on fire with their lusts —

        then this:
                inside an old photo: me

                and in me: her:

                        already we are occupied with
Estrangements:

                        straddling the tricycle,
                                clutching the handlebars,

Veering forward,
                        chin as spire —

Entering (creating) a breach in the waiting — our histories
                        recurring, repeating,
                                (rescinding) themselves —

                        already our pedals thrum —
                                wheels accelerate —
Rise above foreclosure,
                        beyond plane and mulberry tree,

                        up, up,   past

Yew and oak —
                        whip of wind — loosening of light —
Shore to ship —
                        already escape is our

Plight (plan) —

It is September:
        a day bruised by heat,
                        a continent
Reddened with forebodings of shorn head and torch,
                        blued with futures
                                        doomed to die

In frozen squares, gas-filled halls, foodless dorms —

Tell me:

        who will lean over frayed books to chant
Unanswerable prayers —
        who will restrain an uncle's hand before he
Punctures an eardrum to beat the draft —
        who will name a uniformed lover luring her to Buenos Aires,
One whose photo brittled in the drawer —

Nearly her mate, nearly the agent of my never having been —
        and who will confirm the step-mother's
Evil —
                that witch who hid food for her own blood,
Ambushed loaves of bread behind doors,
                        between blankets, in old chests? —

        who will remember what to forget —

                who will
Repair warped porches, chipped windows,
                        stir up Leninist-Trotskyite
Tempests over *schnapps* in the inn —

                who will
Hang on for dear life despite potatoes going bad
                and Poles going mad with rabid rancors —

        who will acknowledge
                        things of darkness as their own?

"Send my regards to Khane and write me from the ship —
may you live and be well,
may you be blessed with good health,
may you have a safe trip,
may you be strong and courageous like
Esther, devoted as Ruth, like Sarah know how to have a good laugh —

may you prosper in New York, may you
Eat chicken and beef three times in the week,
May you light candles each Friday, may you find an hour
to read a good book, may you earn
Enough for yourselves and my grandchildren —

yet not fail to spare
something for us — please G-d —
the ones you have left" —

the ones who will become history without medical
Data or antecedent, losing birth dates, faces,
anecdotes of what they ate,
how they played — whether they
Fought or fantasized, defecated or prayed
as their lungs sponged gas —

whether their hearts were punctured or
Engorged,

if their shrieks
Rang in the crowded silence, if their moans
crashed against mute walls of ill-humored rooms —

unarmed, unblessed —

CHOSEN —

Victims of openings forever closed, redactors
Of the latest version of How To:

how to be TRAPPED, how to be
UNDERLINED FOR EXTERMINATION

while a husband and wife
Rubbed a few coins together in America —

Letters: the shoebox is one-third full of letters;

photos: a worn leather folder hugs in its
Entrails a small packet:

friends and relations never named —

Strangers —

because one couple, safe in America,
tried to forget —
or not to remember —
they had
Survived —

and of those who remained in Poland:
only three:

A sister-in-law who screwed her way
out of danger,
her husband, his brother,
handsome and lazy as hell,
and one nephew,
under-
Sized and overactive,
who, after the war,
needed,

needed too much —
or more than they could give —

that tells
It —

flawed, surmised, and true.

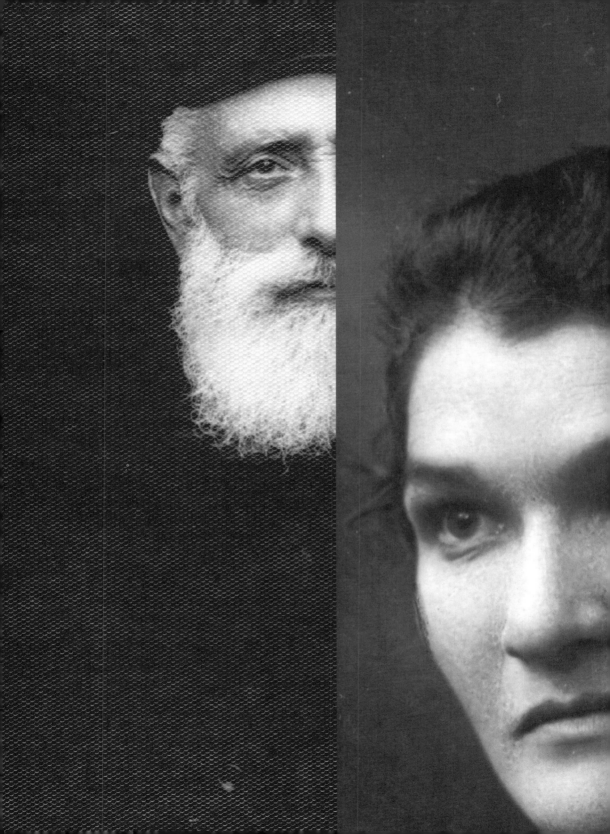

Among remains —
        the story builds — another and another —

        then another —

        as if from a safekeeping —

          this mute parade of faces —
Tongues frozen in a dead of sepia —

        profiles, three-quarters, head-
Ons of unpowderable nose, unshavable chin —

        without
Name —
        without
Context —

      permanently impermanent,

        imperfectly true —

              this one
Endlessly fixed on possibility, a single ringlet

At her brow:

>> — *zum Abiken Andanken,*
>>> Ostroleka, 1918
>> — *remember me forever* —

>> and this one —
>>> no more than twenty,
>> perched on a ladder
>>> in an orchard,
>>>> pretending to pick apples:

>> — *I give you my photo, remember me* —

>>> now in taffeta,
>> turning toward the

View:

>> woods-that-were or may-have-been —
>>> — *life is a battle, so fight to win* —
>>>> — *my photo in remembrance* —
>>> — *for the cousin I love, 1922* —

>> and another, and another:

Our friend, we give you this photo —

>> — *remember us forever,* Warsaw, 1932 —
>>> — *remember me* —
>>>> — *remember I wished you the best* —
>> *from me, Isaac,*
>>> *from me, Helena, Regina, Frank,*
>>>> *from me*
>>>>> *and me,*
>>>>> Ostroleka, 1936 —

>> *and me...*
>>> ·

Is it re-entry they are after,
>> is it markers for their graves,
> is it to remind us they burned
>> with the best possible light,

or is it to urge us to complete them —

"as they were... in great strong masses...

buttons are lost, but clothing remains;
Clothing is lost but figures remain;
figures are lost, but shadows remain;
shadows are lost but the picture remains,
and that,
night cannot
Efface..."

After their fact, after their thought, after their flesh —

Fotographja

Rafael, Lomza — Foto Bekker, Brok —
Cartolina Postale — Postkarte —
Briefkart — Tarjeta Postal —
Carte Postale — Pocztówka —

a little boy in a sailor suit clutches a ball — a young girl
smells a rose —
two women rest heads in their hands,
a third holds a drawstring purse —

a couple
lean against a plant stand,
a child
and a balustrade —

a man in high collar and striped tie —

a woman with blond hair cascading
to her waist —

beside a jagged shore: —

Once I had a love and I was loved —

my mother in a deckchair —

SS Hamburg —

wearing a fur-trimmed coat and a dark cloche

Edged with contrasting trim in a scallop motif —

but I've been left here
Abandoned and alone —

Masha peeking at me between hand-colored fronds
Of a potted palm —

a cottage in a distance of clouds nearing

Naomi in a lace dress — Moishe in a homburg —

Hersh in uniform —

Group photo:

friends — they must be friends —

twenty-four young men and women,
arms entwined —

three rows of eight —

most likely on an outing —
in the mountains —

just having finished
or just before

singing their songs —

"This paper life!
How I hate this paper life!"

Espoused: a woman: 26,
      blue eyes too deep in her cheeks,
      a.k.a. *farkrimpt*, tense — sans *joie*

        a man: 26,
      gray eyeflame in his face,
      a.k.a. *mazik* — mischiefmaker

       espoused:
By her to lament mirrors, by him to be illegible...

    "I've made a mistake, and you,
    what a price you've paid!"

       and for what — for what?

Love? Was it for love?
             pity?
             wanderlust?

      was it
Exhaustion from sparring with dreams
             hitched to their hides?

America, America...*"You haven't been to America!*
         You haven't slaved in a hat
         factory on Broome Street!

         What can you
Know?"

    din, filth, choke of cloth,
           needle prick at her skin,
    treadle beat at her feet,

Three thicknesses of calico coated with shellac...

"We don't know each other!"

    hot irons, brims pried down over crowns
           pulled, dressed, polished,
           lined with China silk…

      "America in exchange for your life?"

           Mr. Bad Luck speeds ahead of her:
           "My ship took ten days, his took three."

           Mr. Bad Luck thumbs his nose at her:
           "What? you want a job that pays more?"

           Mr. Bad Luck dares her to fly:
           "Pack up," he says, *"Run to Poland, Chicago,*
           New York — wherever you like.

I'll find you anywhere. I'll
Get there first."

      "We don't know each other!

      We've only just met!"

           Mr. Bad Luck a brick at her side:

      "He loves my plumage, my
Scent in green air, my habit
Of riding on one leg…

      We'll be a threesome
      when you come because I glut
Vacancies with his name.
           He'll be our staff, our deliverance, our
Educator par excellence…

      We don't know each other!"

Rozowka, hele sitka, tunkele sitka, bekenbroyt —
      gray as bleached rye, black as burnt corn —

      "without him I am lonely, forlorn…"

Hero without a script for romance, heroine with lines
Enjambed despite birds perched on her tongue.

Agreed: to be coupled until
Death:
        to be angry,
               to be loyal,
                      never to know why.

If we suffer for our sins, forgive us;
        if we suffer for the sins of others, pity the in-
Nocent — their silences — nightmarish —
Ablaze with questions driven from the front lines —
           embattled by
Fusillades of sound:

> *"Why must I lie beneath you?*
> *Why must I bear your child?"*

Unspeakable syllables
Leaked from her pen...

THE PURPOSE OF MARRIAGE IS UNION

Language totters from one tongue to another:
How many times will her heart stop?:
> *"...a tempest batters my skull...*
> *why do you call me 'woman of the turned-down mouth'?"*

and what about him? does anyone hear?:
> *"Don't claim marriage is bankrupt...*
> *Don't say you made a mistake..."*

        Backstage, futile attempts
Eavesdrop on precise cues for dialogue.
Alibis bleach out; no prompter can be found.

THE PURPOSE OF UNION IS BIRTH

Retorts drift through streams of ink:

> *"When I get to America we will be together...*
> *we will sign our names in a better light..."*

Truth has not yet been invented; nothing
Encroaches on falsehoods imagined, falsities composed —

        his hand goes limp — his bones burn cold —
        barely defined lines field the stuttering lips:

"Do I need a new coat for New York? Shall I get
Elke to make us a down quilt?

        — gray twill, double-breasted, with a black
Velvet collar, perhaps? — or silk?

        — should she
Embroider our pillowcases or trim them with braid?"

                THE PURPOSE OF BIRTH IS LEARNING

Night swallows
Scraps of explanation —
Outwitted, the plot retreats, taking
No bows,
Gnashing its teeth —
        implacable, imponderable,
           imperfectly played

        —in medias res, inter alia —
           curtained down...

           THE PURPOSE OF LEARNING IS NOT TO KNOW

Owned by a heat: — *There is something in my heart like a burning*
Fire — shut up in my bones — hear me, hear me —

Joyless in these loitering hours — bring silver spoons, a down quilt,
          a photo of our house — I have fevered for thee
On Orchard Street, on Delancey, on Grand — *and I am weary with*
          holding it in — and I cannot — this burning churning —

Yes — oh, yes — stream unto me, into me — I will marcel
          my hair, rouge my cheeks, moisten my lips —
I will put a new song in my mouth — I will plant high trees
          in your ear —

Latebloomers rally to light — *pent up in my bones* — I will
          filigree air —
Like a burning fire — roaring in flight — come quickly from the ship —

I will co-sign your flank, I will ghostwrite your loins —
My heart, lynx-eye of hope — bring a silk blouse blazing with
          rose, a wool scarf lusty with green.

I am weary with holding it in —and I cannot— if my fever-tongue
          knew how to speak —
There is something in my heart — bring opera glasses, a coral brooch,
          buttons wild with bone —

Engulfed by this heat — swollen — flaring — this waiting thickened,
          brambled with heat —
Do you hear me — *locked up in my bones* — will you know me —
          shall I row to you, flame to your boat —

A single hope: you will come
            a single fear: you will not

Night favors the face of the deep,
And I am afflicted with this spectacular need

God be with you, son-in-law, in this hour...

Each morning braced for heavy squalls...

                a speed of threat across the waters...

Doves know no rest for the soles of their feet

                YOU MUST COME

                        I will not let
Thee sail, except I bless thee:

Honor thy father that thy days may be long

            you cannot
Rearrange the Pleiades or loosen the bands of Orion
                        but you can come, you can come...

            how will it look for
Us if you do not

Stranger and sojourner,
                as were all our fathers,
            you shall return no more to your
House, neither shall your place know you anymore, neither your
Face nor your name, bridegroom, nor the
Route of your feet stepping out of your chamber...

And the Lord give thee peace
In climates of sun-
Light spliced by wind,
                in echoes of birdsong,

                                        though the
Garden has lost its youth and times wax old

And the Lord is not in the wind
                    nor in the earthquake
                                    nor in the fire:

        and below the fire
Unreadable faces, inaudible mouths crowd around...

Nameless came they out of their mothers' wombs and nameless
Travail they back...

As a bird to his mountain

                            in the late
Noon of the text

                        you will go
Down to the sea in
Ships and do business
                        in great waters

        WE WILL NEVER SEE EACH OTHER AGAIN

My child, there are no buses, no carriages
                from Brok to Ostroleka, but you must find
A way   scout a way...

                Dear G-d   Dear G-d

Langer tzeit nisht zehn   long time no see

Long time no see

In the dead desire of then and there
in the unclaimed country strewn with pasts

Narratives stripped of detail
contexts shorn of history

Brevities burrowing through frozen dreams
syllables unrooting in icy screams

Lives owning less and less of themselves
we are living as if in a war

Archival dwindle
liquified prayer

Shunted from one stillbirth to another
O why are embryos wrenched from our wombs

Tragedies commuted from first stops to dead ends
trains profane being without to being erased

Barbers strop razors
the honed tracks agleam

50

Erasures of hair
the surfeit of flesh

Reason closes down
bereaved skies opaque

Unending hungers, absent beds, blank walls
when the sun scours the earth it will go blind

Faith graying — O excrement of ash
months with no news, send clothing, send food

Fluent with anecdote torn from their mouths
nouns orphaned by verbs gone blood-raving mad

Locutions of this are not — cannot be — that
there are times a letter means more than money

Enigmas fuel the lines, the smudged borders
we fled to Ostrov, to Tsekanovtze, to...

Dossiers begging escape to the grave
today father died of these privations

Particles of data unable to testify
how can we tell of our sufferings, our wanderings

Laconic forests galloping words
do not abandon us, hear our pleas

Unrobed for the shadows
naked where lost days roil

Mossy maneuvers — half-taught, half-lived lives
worms fuss with our bones, crows yearn for our eyes

Embers now thirsting for flame
there are no Jews left in Brok...

"How good it is,
         dear children,
                  that you are settled"

A man, a woman growing gaps

"Decent rooms,
         nice furniture, and
                  meat once each week"

Coated with unslaked desire

"Here in Ostroleka,
         God's been absent
                  all winter"

Out of range regrets explode

"Stones and snow
         pelt Poles who
                  trade with Jews"

Eye to eye with guilts and another year

"Nat sent $5. And you? Have
         you forgotten to love us?
                  your father, Shlomo C."

"To my dear brother and sister-in-law,
Have you been gone so long to write so little?
Upon our knees, we beseech you — do not become
Strangers, keep us informed...
Taste our cries, touch our fires
                  do not mention us in passing —

Our screams — wild for our shadows —
                  (surely they did not intend their leave-taking?)
         tumble from us like unstrung beads

Forget nothing of this:

> *we are starved, jobless, terrified,*
>
> *Lately of elsewhere, lured to nowhere—*
>
> > *pity our skins, our*
> *Impotent bones,*
>
> > *pray for yourselves and for us, too...*
>
> *Naked as we*
> *Grovel for / grapple with / God —*
>
> > *pray for us... pray for us...*
>
> > *I kiss you with all my shattered heart...*
> > *your sister, Royzeh M. "*

"Hear this, hear this, dear brother, Feivel the tailor turns old overcoats
Inside out and makes them new.

Ship your discards, rejects— any outer garments—
> *to get us through winter.*
> > *from me, Moishe"*

Salvage of coats —

> this Coat which is Nightmare

> this Mantle   this Shroud

> this Coat which is Map
Of a Coat inflicted on them

> > Coat of Ruins

> > Coat of Fear

> > Nomad Coat

Unable to shield —

I AM COLD IN THIS COAT

this Tattered Need Without Lining,

this Flag of Flight   this Ravel of Pain

Wrapper of Traces
in which shoulders slope

Riptide of Sleeves

Maelstrom of Cuffs

unhemmed

Landscape

Makeshift Hiding Place

Running Place

stitched and unstitched

abandoned by thread

Upon a time   hardened regions
    once a time   ambushed

        red-coal teeth bared   lethal sun
        gnaws cloth at his loins
        tatters   rain pellets stain
        gray   puce   brown

Parsnips   ONCE   a time
    buff-colored   firm   sweet tasting

        "that man"   nailed to withered wood   SHAMELESS
        each winter battered by careening cacophanies of weather
        shattered eyes fixed on evidence   rusty tongs   spear
        hammer thumping on rotted cross

Opportunities of orange   marbled beef   broadcloth   spilling
    from bolts   bolting   from spills

        in spring   air uncurdled
        churchyard cordoned with young girls
        saints cradled in their arms   streamered bonnets
        flame-red skirts   syllabled silver   gold

Nuances of baby's breath   gnawed by clouds

        cascading phrases of long yellow
        braid   satin robes   priestly
        beneath a jewel-tasseled canopy
        as April conjugates budding meadows

Tremble   O black fields
Harnessed to history   believers
Ejaculate entreaties into bloody
Gardens stripped of transaction   lilies lie rancid...
Rare doves lust for promises of armature

                            incomplete wings beached
On the (t)errors of flight

56

in the cauldron of spring   deep
as wells of longed-for words   wide as the circumference
of heart's fear   louder   louder   women's chants
higher   higher   smoke rives river   hills   streets

Walled up   whelmed in the unutterable
Incised   in the unforgettable
Nightmare   of nothing   and notbeing

indecipherable hieroglyphs   hurled this hour
at two thousand Jews in the *shtetl*   *az men*
klingt   when church bells ring   *goyim*
have a holiday   WHEN THERE'S SMOKE   there's fire

Grammar of ashword   syntax of howl
Gematria drowned in
Liquid numbers   ink-stained   illegible gestures...

men twitch as they rock to *marev* prayers   women dizzy
their lips with whatever psalms they recall
behind bolted doors   shielded by *mezuzahs*
families huddle   clutch the book they deem holy

Only
Once
    upon a time missing in action

Mountained in history

ears clogged   eyes closed   mouths shut
in empty numbed streets   the barely
audible tremor of tongues   *"dear god*
let us not suffer   forgive us   forgive us"

1946

DEC 4

BROOKLYN

JUL 22 1946 (64TH. ST. STA.) BROOKLYN N.Y.

N.Y.

8317

Bro

NEW YORK
7·2
194
REG'Y.

YORK

Pas recla

20 ave

klyn N. Y.

n. S. A.

BROOKLYN N. Y.

DEC
1940

S. A.

G. SEC. TOU

POZNAŃ

S

8 45 14

*

*

nie poożk

207 VIII

So little cause, and illusions of meaning withdraw.
O little cause of timetorn torntime motes in time,
Little can they know trapped in that time,
In that abyss of history when wordclaws

Tear at their throats, when an alphabet — hell-sent
To taverns of steaming samovars, hell bound —
Lies in wait, not knowing when, how, why peril may sound —
Elbows into the marketplace, jostles the remnant

Crowds — Moishe the Barber, resident now of silence,
Apostle of naked chins, shaves the peasant faces,
Unbeards the Jews who have strayed —
Simon the Merchant mans three carts at once —

Edifice of fur hat, hill of velvet frock, pyramid of boot,
                              and in New York "Little
Flower" reads the comics, swings a baton at Carnegie Hall,
On his motorcycle rushes as if tomorrow can be stalled,
Rushes in his sidecar to the latest fire, has faith that evil,

Culpabilities are temporary alliances with darkness,
Antipathies slated to be erased from the moral terrain,
Rounds the corner on the glittering, unstoppable wheels of better days,
On a roll, on the march, speeding through expectant, hope-doused streets —

Little causes: skullcaps, sideburns, leaning cottages on chicken legs —
If we forget— lest we forget—O scattered sheep exiled to lost roads,
Nuggets of piety cling to their coats, on their brows they glow — O
Guardian light — on the floor a child writhes, the *rebbe's* in the stove —
Slumber, *landsleit* doze — long live this drone,
                              this winterdark of dregs...

OFFICIAL ANNOUNCEMENT: we proudly report a new technique for site-
     specific articulation of negative space: a groundbreaking
Framework for transforming a visual field of breathing referents into a
Space metamorphosed to ambiguity by a seething landscape laced with
     nostalgia.

Under a capacious sun, at approximately 9 a.m., we reclaimed the paved
     square —
Corners where *Ostrov, Worynska, Sporynska* and *Ulinits* intersect.
Hundreds of Jews were laid face up in a grid-like pattern.
Enticements to the eye were provided by wobbly reliefs of bodies on
Cobbled stone, while demeanors of kinesthesia were achieved by
Subtle heaves of supine form, the writhe of which we labored
To contain with bayonets and rifle butts lest the undulating
Abstraction lapse into chaos, lest this *never to be written page of honor
     in our history* be marred.

Troubled by such unchecked textures, our heroic men, *decent and hard
     throughout,* chiseled the hobnails of their boots
Into the assemblage, and when, from time to time, the design, as artistic
Creations are often known to do, declared itself, emitting tremors,
     shivers, sometimes garbled, gutteral

Sound, our expert craftsmen, with iron bars and wooden planks, with
      diagonal sweeps of gestural swagger
Orchestrated across the surface, restored order, rendering blood as
      rivulets and thin washes,
Urine as cursive jottings, mucus and excrement as heavily encrusted
      impastoes and edgy spills resistant to closure.
Noteworthy, too, was our palette: broad fillips of color: celadon to
      amber to ruby and blue.

Domination Theory, Pure Imagery, and Plastic Arts at last united in a
      grand graffiti of spectatorship and alienation defying depletion.

LISTENERS: IMAGINE WHERE SUCH INNOVATION MAY TAKE US!

Whittled regions, watery seasons
A landscape never to be read
                              or rewritten

                    if they had hammered nails to our gums
                              and not cut off our hands

                                                            Dayenu

"Such joy we had this Sabbath eve
When your letter arrived after five months"

Raw eyes rime the wracked roads

                    if they had sliced off Moishe's lids
                              and not forced Khaneh to eat them

                                                            Dayenu

If forgetting is a death...
The urgency to remember a walling up...

Their marks:
                              canvas of shadow
                                             palette of dung
Erosrattle in their groins

"Nekheh, Meyer and Soreleh moved in with us"

"On Sukkes your mother had a heart attack"

"Nathan, the baker, owes Hershl for a bale of flour"

"Tevyeh Khaneh Khaye's offered five zlotys for each dollar you sent...
Even Yossel, the fool, knows they give seven for one right here on my street"

                    if they had shorn arms from the children
                              and not choked the wind with their necks

                                                            Dayenu

"Rokhl and Hershl are in Tshekhanovtse

Rivke Malke's and Yossel in Zembrova

Ephraim in Vilna, Alter, your father, in Sokolke

Shmilke an orderly in Minsk

Tevye in Tashkent"

        O starstammer, smoke-
Roar, trains race to deceit.

        if they had crushed us on broken glass
            and not hollowed our eyes with bayonets
                    Dayenu

"I rolled the zlotys in my hand and flung them to the floor"

*"An action in Khelm: firemen smashed the roofs of our
Landsmen's stores while they prayed"*

        if they had twisted screws in Soreh's legs
            and not ripped the lips from Faigel's face
                    Dayenu

These are the generations of Ostroleka, of Brok, of
HELL on earth

In the days when
No skins radiated,
        having spoken with Him,

    when
God
Slept in

        as ifs begat and begat and begat

                    Dayenu

And no voice and charred leaves ungathered

                                    implacable
Fragments grass the tracks

                    have you seen the woman

                        fixed at every station

                    peering left   *then right*

                        finally crossing the tracks

At the sites of blame where breaths accrued

Repeating the craned neck

                the desperate eye

                        making haste again to another side

O the maimed acres   the fiefdoms of those

                and irretrievable days

Racing away

NOTHING IS MORE REAL THAN NOTHING

In the diaspora of sparks

                        the woman stoops for every shard

Guards each rift   between betweens

                the woman I am lonely within

Hearing mainly the hiss of ancient hates
And the incessant throbbing of tongues
Raped by the hard truths

have you seen her fondling the traces

have you watched her fumbling for names

On hands and knees digging to
Unearth words
Native to no language

O woman on your odyssey to no
Destination

you must stumble

you must stumble

these stumbling blocks in your hands

are in

your hands

your hands are in

in

The mind is its own place:
Hier ruhen alle Tote:

                    nomads bearing cinders

                              evidence

               which is the taste of whither

               the sting of why

Adrift in an overture
                    On-
The-Way

               whose sighted landings
                         are but momentary
Islands in immense fictions which court the ports

Country of Orphaned Silhouettes...

               City of Cloud...

Outpost of Crowded Griefs

Ultima Thule of Shutdown Skies...

               what do you know about
Liquidated futures or bones

Denied ground?

                         she cannot find

Their ground, nor the fate of their bones...

Hungering through the lists for their names...

In the granulating dark...

No echo nourishes the ravening or sounds an inaugural
Knell in the *Appelplatz:*

> nothing brings them near...

> *no, no, no*
> *THEY WILL COME NO MORE...*

Home of Tangled Obscurities

> what use are you
> whose center flames

Everywhere

> whose circumference
> is a nowhere choked with trails...

Region where unreason tethers the missing parts...

> they will not step into
Extinction with inklings they were

> *SHE CANNOT STEP AWAY...*

Terrain of Unanimous Night...

he waits for loaves to
Rise, measures butter, eggs,
Each morning kneads, slaps, slams dough on
Marble slabs, coaxes limp wads to shapely
                    rounds of rye, mounds of black
Bread crowned with floured domes...

THEY WILL COME NO MORE...

Landscape of Ghost-swarm...

"our father died of marches, our mother of an

Enormous inhale..."

Domain of Shadows
                    wrangling with once-there-was
                        and never-again...

Territory of Havens trapped behind lids...

                    no footfall in the
Halls...

Realm where what we say about things
                        dishonors the facts

                    they could not dye the world their own color

Outback of Unwriting

meaning unknown

meaning
undone...

Underground of Lacerated Mouths...

each poem is a
Grave.....

I CANNOT MAKE ENOUGH POEMS

the mind shapes neither
Heaven nor Hell

the mind is its own place...

Here I invent them:

In the early century

                              in the heat of late August

        (waiting to be sung)

        rowing their boat   on the Narew   the Bug

                        (loathing their loneliness)

Slant into spanglewaters

            (O wander-full air)

Horizons of hopebrood

            (heralding gulls)

       how they hanker after those

                going   going   gone

                (hoard of simmer there)

Abandon your skies

        (but not your souls)

          refit your pasts

     reject your God

          (dare I say it?)   of dead salutations

                                                (O God who flickered once)

            but not your songs

                                        not the
Presage of change

Press

                    press into it

                                not away

            (they are in their twenties)
                            a melody rises like
Yeast in the latent direction

                                    (among initials)

            they seek words for it

Good day   good night

Open to them   for them   with them
                            into their

Orphanhood

Drawn to the decoding

                (the upstream not oared before)

                    into an endless, superior

Need

72

In the seethe of late August

                      (after the Great War)

Gunfire has invaded his right thigh

                      Cossackfire

Has hovelled her house

They are rife with what they lose to live new lives

Anchored in my afterthought

(In which they do not age)

              (in which they wait their singing)

                  (now late in the century)

                            in which

Raptors ride

Sing slender songs   *stillness where silence crouches*

Overgrown codas and stabs at the past   *abandoned and alone*
Move a bit of air   *each poem is a prayer*

Every day a new an-other, a bruised
        ignorance   *in this difficulty*
Bleeds from me containing   *among shards*
Losses and the long dead I did not know

Even those and what I touched   *what did it mean to live a life*
        not stirring now   *what the color of day of*
                                             thought of unsealed lips

Streetcars on Bath Avenue mounds   *of shade and baffled dreams*
        of rust and rot
Smokechoked incinerators'   *an infant lies in the bathroom sink*
        stale fume-roam   *she is clean but unfed she does not*
                                             grow or learn to smile she is me she
                                             is my mother we are starving to death

Entreaties claw out of coverage

Distances stretch broad at the gate   *the sun was black*
                                             the sun was destruction

Having forgotten the way back, hooked
On posterity with its incipience erased

I will meet you in the wordless
downpour of abouttobe
I will listen for you in the
thunder of arrival

People are afraid to look at each other

POEMS STARE INTO THEIR EYES

Eternity chews on the facts

if these words were assigned
taste they would be dungfire
bonemoulder   ashbreeze

With their worn-down shoes, their
Hungry sleeves were they always
       bodies conceding their needs
       could be reduced;
          with their
Errands and knapsacks their collars like
      nooses, not one rock
Rests above their mouths, not one
      stone at the

gribenes *and onions*
tsibelleh *and* schmaltz

"your sister Rosie and her
family are living in very bad
material conditions"

Ear, no pebble where eyes might have
      peered skyward

did they know they inhabited
the limits of the possible

O you who begged for a letter
      O you who did not write

did they know mulberry trees
push out leaves all summer
did they try to reconvene
the starry sky

Faster, faster, bits of air, with fine excess
Hurry into the arena;
Entropy dwells in the dust

"we received your package:
970 grams cocoa 950 grams
fat 970 grams dry tea 700
grams soup 960 grams rice
980 grams coffee a total of 5
kilograms 76 grams my dears
thank you from the bottom of
our hearts"

75

Keep the omnivore at bay, delay the
        abductor
Night and day on call to
Exchange fact for lie
Wick for light

the words draw away from me I did not want
to be alone with them if they were there
they did not want to be alone with me they were eyes
of strewn blear they were high ears they were mouths
that chewed silence
they were noses breathing ash

before the need for God was the need to pray

each poem is a prayer

Song-stripped
Oblivion
Mires
Evidence

Battered
Legacies

Ergo

Sightless
Starshine
Exfoliating
Dishevelled
Heaven

O outstretched
Plenitude
Emanating
Waste

Here
Endless
Refugees
Emigrate
On
Foot

Here
Eveningnoonmorningnight
Knows
No
Earthly
Waltz

As if as then as when a heaviness lightens as
Now I remember I breathe a breath of you each
Day I remember as then you were with me in August
In Brok sun kindled the pines circling the river
Water flowed warm I rocked on the porch
And watched you swim like a perch you like a fish
Swept back and forth just like a fish now tears
Undo you my life is worth no more than a dishrag
No more than a crumb Soreleh is at my side she bears
A leaf a pencil some paper she has found a leaf these
Words are stone she has brought one leaf
And the water was warm now syllables drown in these
Rivers a leaf yellow and orange still speckled with green
Expelled from the garden sky-deep the debris

A
N
D

I

W
A
S

U
N
A
W
A
R
E

The Darkling Thrush

I leant upon a coppice gate
    When frost was spectre-gray,
And Winter's dregs made desolate
    The weakening eye of day.
The tangled bine-stems scored the sky
    Like strings of broken lyres
And all mankind that haunted nigh
    Had sought their household fires.

The land's sharp features seemed to be
    The Century's corpse outleant,
His crypt the cloudy canopy,
    The wind his death-lament.
The ancient pulse of germ and birth
    Was shrunken hard and dry,
And every spirit upon earth
    Seemed fervourless as I.

At once a voice arose among
    The bleak twigs overhead
In a fullhearted evensong
    Of joy illimited:
An aged thrush, frail, gaunt, and small,
    In blast-beruffled plume,
Had chosen thus to fling his soul
    Upon the growing gloom.

So little cause for carolings
    Of such ecstatic sound
Was written on terrestrial things
    Afar or nigh around,
That I could think there trembled through
    His happy good-night air
Some blessed Hope, whereof he knew
    And I was unaware.

Thomas Hardy
(January 1, 1900)

Darkling is a book-length sequence which utilizes the 32 lines of "The Darkling Thrush" by Thomas Hardy as its acrostic armature. Thus, when read down its extreme left-hand margin, each segment spells out a line, in consecutive order, of "The Darkling Thrush." The last two lines of Hardy's poem are repeated, making a total sequence of 34 segments. In some cases the acrostic structure is evident; in others there is so much fragmentation that the armature is barely apparent. Nevertheless, the acrostic as framework, generative power and resonance remained important to me throughout the writing.

Why acrostics, and why "The Darkling Thrush?"

For a number of years I had been haunted by my inheritance of truncated histories, sketchy memories, bits of narrative, and the contents of a shoebox containing old photos and letters that had been translated for me from Yiddish into English. I found myself also haunted by "The Darkling Thrush"—by its tone of millennial mourning, by its note of hope in the thrush's song, and most especially by its opening line which situates the poet as he meditates on the passing century: "I leant upon a coppice gate." I, too, felt as if I was peering into a coppice—a wood or thicket characterized by a dense, often tangled, underwood of stump shoots and suckers encouraged into being by the periodic cutting down of trees. At the same time, I had been experimenting with acrostics, exploring the possibility of their constraint to generate new constructs of language, all the while wondering if the ancients were on to something in their belief in the mystical power of the acrostic form. And so, the idea of an acrostic sequence was born.

P. 19: The question at the end, "...why were you not you?" makes reference to the 17th century mystic, Zusya of Annapol, who lived a life of wandering, poverty and inwardness, and is reported to have said: "In the next world I will not be asked 'Why were you not Moses, but why were you not Zusya?'"

P. 24: The italicized couplet at the end is from *Ecclesiastes:* 10:20.

P. 25: References are made to the Proclamation of the Central Committee of the Jewish Labor Bund which was issued after the Kishinev pogrom in March 1903 and to *Deuteronomy* 4:34: "with a mighty arm."

The Bund, founded in 1897, was an organization which appealed to the common Jewish people because it supported national and cultural autonomy for them within Polish society, because of its exclusively Yiddishist bent, and because its explicit secularism embodied traditional Jewish values. It extolled physical resistance and preparedness to fight if necessary for its convictions. This contrasted with the Rabbinic tradition, which was considered aristocratic and patrician, the Haskala movement, which was viewed as too bookish, upper class and snobbish, and with Zionism, deemed bourgeois and philanthropic, and which, by proposing emigration to Palestine, had succumbed to the pressures of living in the Diaspora by, in a sense, giving up.

Nina Berberova in a *New Yorker* interview in 1960: "All my life I was preoccupied with time which can neither be bought, nor stolen, nor faked."

P. 27: In 'Cosmology': The reference is to Isaac ben Solomon Luria (1160-1235), the famous Hasid whose insights were believed to have been based on interior, rather than terrestrial sightings.

P. 29: 'Destiny' appropriates phrases from *Isaiah* 41:18 and 62:4 by way of George Eliot's *Daniel Deronda*.

P. 40: The quotation which begins "as they were" and ends "night cannot / Efface" is from the notebooks of James McNeill Whistler.

P. 47: I am indebted here to Rilke's *Sonnets to Orpheus*, to *Psalms* 40:3: "And he hath put a new song in my mouth," and to *Lamentations*.

P. 48: This segment is laced throughout with paraphrases of and quotations from the *Old Testament*—all in an attempt to speak in the voice of the father who was an *elul*, a class of lay persons of very high intelligence whose scholarly inclinations were supported by the Polish *shtetl* community.

P. 60: "Little Flower" was the nickname of Fiorello LaGuardia, the legendary mayor of New York City.

P. 61: Reference is made here to a speech made by S.S. Reichsführer Heinrich Himmler to a meeting of S.S. generals in Posen on October 4, 1943:

> I also want to speak very frankly about an extremely important subject. Among ourselves we will discuss it openly; in public, however, we must never mention it…I mean the evacuation of the Jews, the extermination of the Jewish people…Most of you know what it is to see a pile of one hundred or five hundred or one thousand bodies. To have stuck it out and at the same time, barring exceptions caused by human weakness, to have remained decent: this is what has made us tough…
>
> This is a glorious page in our history which never has and never will be written.

P. 63: "Dayenu" appears in the Passover *Haggadah*. It means "it would have been enough," and is chanted by the Seder participants after each of God's favors is recited.

Throughout *Darkling* featherings, hatchings, bleeds, filaments, drips and daubs from Paul Celan; *An Interrupted Life* by Etty Hillesum; Lawrence Langer's *Admitting the Holocaust, The Holocaust and the Literary Imagination, Holocaust Testimonies,* and *Art From the Ashes; My Century* by Aleksander Wat; *The Old Testament; Zakhor* by Yosef Yerushalmi as well as his *Freud's Moses; The Essential Kabbalah* by Daniel C. Matt; *The Survivor* by Terence Des Pres; *Life is With People* by Mark Zborowski and Elizabeth Herzog; *Treblinka* by Jean-Francois Steiner; George Steiner; *The Jews in Polish Culture* by Aleksander Hertz; Walter Benjamin; Isaiah Berlin; Danilo Kis; Franz Kafka; Samuel Beckett; Rainer Maria Rilke; *The Song of Songs;* Heinrich Heine; Gershom Scholem's *The Origins of the Kabbalah; The Emigrants* and *The Rings of Saturn* by W.G. Sebald; Isaac Babel's *1920 Diary; From a Ruined Garden,* Jack Kugelmass and Jonathan Boyarin, editors; *European Jews in Two Worlds,* Deborah Moore, editor; *On the Edge of Destruction* by Celia S. Heller; *The Jews in Poland,* edited by Cleiman Abransky, Macief Jachemczyk, and Antony Polonsky; *The Literature of Destruction,* edited by David Roskies; *The Gifts of the Jews* by Thomas Cahill; *1939, The Lost World of the Fair* by David Gelernter and more and more and more…